IMAGES O

Canning Town

IMAGES OF ENGLAND

Canning Town

Howard Bloch
and
Nick Harris

NONSUCH

Cover photograph: Hoy Street. One of the photographs taken by George Taylor of the Silver Jubilee celebrations on 6 May 1935. See also pages 78 and 79.

First published 1994
This new pocket edition 2005
Images unchanged from first edition

Nonsuch Publishing Limited
The Mill, Brimscombe Port,
Stroud, Gloucestershire, GL5 2QG
www.nonsuch-publishing.com

British Library Cataloguing in Publication Data
A catalogue record for this book is available from the British Library

ISBN 1-84588-136-2

Typesetting and origination by Nonsuch Publishing Limited
Printed in Great Britain by Oaklands Book Services Limited

Contents

Introduction

Although the origin of the name Canning Town remains uncertain, settlement began on the low-lying marsh in the early 1840s. The opening of the railway line and C.J. Mare's shipbuilding works in 1846, the Victoria Dock in 1855 and a number of chemical industries created a demand for housing. Two new towns, Canning Town and Hallsville, grew up to accommodate the workers and their families. Rapid and uncontrolled, this development lacked a proper water supply and sewerage system and experienced the spread of diseases such as cholera and smallpox.

By the 1880s it had become a major centre of industry in the South. People from all over Britain were attracted to the area to work in the factories, docks and Beckton Gasworks. Ships from many lands passed through the docks and seamen often came ashore. Much of the work available was casual and subject to economic and seasonal fluctuations. People could only afford to live in overcrowded and inadequate housing which lacked basic amenities. Pollution, dangerous and unhealthy working conditions and long hours meant that accidents and death were an everyday occurrence. Each new immigrant population which settled there, whether Irish, German, Jewish, Italian or Afro-Caribbean was forced to accept ever worse conditions.

People sought to improve their working and living conditions through trade union and political activities and sought office on West Ham Council and in Parliament. Canning Town became the focus of a number of new movements and several of those involved, including Will Thorne and James Keir Hardie, became leading figures in the Labour Party. Amongst the women who played a significant part in the struggles were Eleanor Marx, Sister Edith Kerrison, Daisy Parsons and Sylvia Pankhurst. These people shaped the new services provided by West Ham Council, especially those concerned with housing, health and welfare.

Voluntary organisations such as churches, hospitals and charities were also very active in the area, especially during the early 1900s. This was a period marked by widespread unemployment and distress which was compounded by the closure of the area's main employer, the Thames Ironworks, in 1912. Settlements such as Mansfield House and the Malvern College Mission were established in Canning Town by a number of public schools and universities whose members lived and worked among the poor.

Between the wars, the inhabitants of Canning Town felt a strong sense of common identity, often helping one another, especially when times were hard. People worked and spent their leisure time together – a visit to the pub, dance hall, boxing or football match was the highlight of their week while an outing to Epping Forest, Southend or a working holiday hop-picking in Kent was something to save for and look forward to.

The Council sought to alleviate some of the worst aspects of housing and poverty through a programme of slum clearance and health promotion. New houses with modern facilities were built and new services including clinics, nurseries and the lido were opened. The long delays faced by traffic were reduced by the construction of the Silvertown Way and the new approach roads to the Docks in the 1930s.

The Second World War brought dramatic changes. Hundreds were evacuated to safer areas or moved away never to return. Despite the dangers, many stayed on and worked for the war effort in the docks, factories and civil defence services. The area was one of the most heavily bombed in Britain and many families suffered tragedy. People who lived through these times felt they deserved a better future for themselves and their families.

Plans were made by West Ham Council for the re-development of Canning Town before the War had ended. The aim was to reduce the number of people who lived there, transfer its industry and build a new neighbourhood unit, the Keir Hardie Estate, which included housing, schools and welfare services. The demand for housing could not be met immediately and many people moved away to new estates in Essex and new towns such as Basildon and Harlow. It was not until the early 1960s that most of the remaining bomb sites were replaced by new houses, shops and a street market.

High-rise living was seen to be a solution to the housing shortage and its benefits were extolled. The skyline changed as many of the terraced houses were swept away and tower blocks went up in their place. The collapse of one of them – Ronan Point, led this social experiment in mass housing to be called into question in Britain and in other parts of the world.

Many of the long-established industries closed during the 1960s and 1970s moved away or reduced their workforce. The Royal Docks, which had provided the base for much of the area's economic activity, closed in 1981.

The sharp rise in unemployment has been reflected by increased levels of poverty, crime and racism coupled with deteriorating housing and health. Run down and neglected the area has seen little benefit from the developments around it, especially those in docklands. Canning Town can never go back to its industrial past but locally-based initiatives might enable its inhabitants to build a new sense of identity for the area.

One

The Barking Road and Old Canning Town

The River Lea flood barrier under construction in 1973. The cooling towers of West Ham power station dominated the Canning Town skyline from the 1950s until their demolition in 1984.

The low-lying marshland on which Canning Town was built has been subject to flooding for thousands of years. Following the disastrous floods in 1953, efforts were made to improve flood defences in the Thames and its tributaries. This drop-gate barrier spanned the loop of the River Lea at Bow Creek. It was demolished in the early 1990s during the construction of the Docklands Light Railway.

Traffic making its way along the Barking Road from Poplar in 1930. The railway lines follow Bow Creek along the banks of which were located a number of wharves including Sankey's, on the right of this picture.

The bridge on the left was built in steel in 1896 by the Thames Ironworks to replace the 'Iron Bridge' which had stood since 1810. The curve of the road made it an awkward approach for horse traffic, especially in wet weather. The bridge marked the boundaries between the old counties of Middlesex on the west and Essex in the east.

The new bridge in 1932. Built in conjunction with the dock approaches scheme, it was opened at the same time as Silvertown Way. Many locals still refer to this modern structure as the 'Iron Bridge'.

This view of the Barking Road in 1930, looking west, shows the old Bridge House public house on the right. When time was called here at 10.00 p.m., many drinkers were seen running across the bridge to the Iron Bridge Tavern, Poplar, where the licensing regulations allowed them an extra half-hour.

The old Bridge House was demolished and replaced in 1930 by a mock-Tudor building when the new bridge and approach roads to the Docks were constructed. In this view from the Barking Road, in 1965, Canning Town station is on the right. One of the cooling towers of West Ham power station can be seen in the background.

Looking west at the Barking Road and Silvertown Way junction in 1965, before the Newham Way and its flyover were built. The Bridge House can be seen on the right and the Imperial Cinema, by then a bingo hall, is visible on the left.

A busy scene in the Barking Road in 1930, looking east. Canning Town station was opened in 1846 on the southern side of the Barking Road and was moved to the northern side in 1888. The building shown was replaced in the course of the Dock Approaches Scheme. The circular urinal stood on the corner of Stephenson Street in front of W.W. Howard's timber yard (see page 63).

The corner of Ship Street and Stephenson Street, *c.* 1900. These houses were built on the marshes around 1850 to accommodate the thousands of workers who came from around the country to work in the new factories and docks. The streets north of the Barking Road between the River Lea and the railway line to North Woolwich, which included Bidder and Stephenson Streets, developed as a distinctive district which became known locally as 'Old Canning Town'.

Many of the Victorian terraced houses in Bidder Street shown here were cleared after this photograph was taken in 1934.

Much of the accommodation in Canning Town was rented and some of the landlords were resistant to carrying out repairs. Most houses had been built without basic amenities such as hot and cold water and an inside bathroom and toilet. The facilities which did exist were often shared between more than one family. The Council served a notice on these houses at 136 and 138 Bidder Street in 1924 because they were in a dangerous condition and had been shored up. The necessary repairs were subsequently carried out.

The western section of the Barking Road, c. 1930. The nearest building on the right is the Imperial Palace Cinema.

An elevated view south along Burnham Street from the Barking Road in 1930. The Liverpool Arms is on the right while Denton and Co. menswear shop is closing down to make way for Silvertown Way. St Luke's Church can be seen across the rooftops on the far left.

Above: Looking east on the north side of Barking Road in 1904. The buildings distinguishable include the London and County Bank, the Thames Ironworks Federated Clubs. The Royal Oak public house, which can be seen in the distance, was made famous in the 1980s by the boxer, Frank Bruno, who trained in its gym.

Right: A view of the same buildings in the Barking Road, looking west, in 1904. The London and County Bank at numbers 51 and 53 became the National Westminster Bank which has recently closed. The Thames Ironworks Federated clubs at number 55 co-ordinated many of the company's social and sporting activities.

A panoramic view looking north from the Barking Road in 1972. Many of the streets seen here, including Liverpool and Malmesbury Roads, were demolished in the 1970s.

Crossing the road at the corner of the Barking Road and Beckton Road in 1965. Local people are well served in this section of the road by a range of shops and the nearby Rathbone Street Market. Amongst the shops here in the 1930s which are still in business today are Granditer's men's outfitters and Murkoff confectioners while Woolworth's closed in 1993.

The photographer captured this everyday scene in Star Lane in around 1900. The chimneys of the houses and factories poured out black smoke and women fought a constant battle to keep their houses clean. A row of terraced houses survives in Star Lane (recently re-named Newhaven Lane) and the fire insurance marks on them can still be seen.

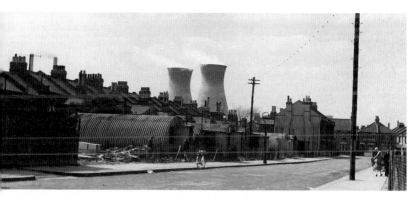

Prefabricated houses known as nissen huts in Blake Road in the 1950s. Although intended as a temporary measure to rehouse those made homeless by bomb damage some were inhabited for over twenty years.

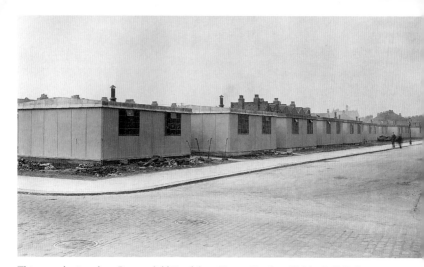

This westerly view along Beaconsfield Road from Hermit Road on 22 March 1945 shows some 'Uni-Seco' pre-fabricated huts.

Beaconsfield Road, *c.* 1950.

Two

South of the Barking Road

Looking south down Victoria Dock Road from the Barking Road in 1931. Amongst the buildings on the left are Samuel Spink's, hairdressers, the cinema and the Town of Ayr public house.

A view of Victoria Dock Road in the 1880s. Canning Town station is on the left and Relf's Music Hall is on the right. Charles Relf opened his music hall in about 1875, and after his retirement as manager in 1906 it became the Royal Albert. It was rebuilt in 1909 partly from materials from the Imperial Theatre, Westminster and re-named the Imperial Theatre and subsequently used as a cinema.

Looking westward at the notorious 'White Gates' level crossing from Victoria Dock Road to Dock Road towards to Silvertown and North Woolwich in 1904. The HMS *Black Prince* is on the stocks of the Thames Ironworks in the background.

This northerly view of Victoria Dock Road includes a large crowd waiting at the 'White Gates'. A number of buildings have recently been demolished to make way for the Jubilee Line extension.

Looking north along Dock Road in 1904. The foot bridge over the railway at the 'White Gates' crossing is in the distance. The queue of traffic is waiting for the gates to open to cross into Victoria Dock Road. The railway to the left is the old North Woolwich line before it was realigned north of the Victoria Dock.

The construction of Silvertown Way from 1932–4 cut a swathe through Canning Town and Tidal Basin. Known as the 'Road to the Empire', the highway and viaduct formed the principal part of the £2½ million scheme to improve the approaches to the Royal Docks. The Thames Ironworks building can be seen in the right background.

This view from September 1933 shows the Silvertown Way under construction.

The opening of Silvertown Way on 13 September 1934. Alderman Herbert J. Rumsey, the Mayor of West Ham, welcomes the Minister of Transport, Leslie Hore-Belisha (who introduced Belisha Beacons to the country).

Right: The demolition of a terrace of houses in Woodstock Street, *c.* 1937. Hundreds of Victorian houses in Canning Town were pulled down in the 1930s, many of which were unfit for human habitation.

Below: Numbers 17 to 27a Swanscombe Street in October 1934 – the year before they were subject to a clearance order. Note the shutters and footscrapers at the front of the houses.

29

Probably the junction of Nelson and Emily Streets, a poor part of the Tidal Basin area near St Luke's Church, *c.* 1925.

The original home of Grimstead's, a name well known in the motor-cycle trade, at the corner of Fisher Street and Beckton Road in 1972.

Above: Prosser Terrace, 13 Beckton Road, 1890.
E. Prosser advertised in the Stratford Almanac
for 1877 as a 'builder and contractor, practical
carpenter and joiner' at 18 Bidder Street. He
built a number of houses in Canning Town
during the 1870s, including this group to which
he gave his name, which were built around 1879.

Right: Numbers 14 and 15 Beckton Road in the
same year.

A panorama of Newham Way development in 1971.

The Newham Way flyover sweeps through the centre of Canning Town in 1972. The Royal Oak public house can be seen through the arches at the left.

Above: Morgan Street, 1954, after the repairs which led to an increase in rent. The tenants claimed they had already been paid for out of a public fund.

Right: Numbers 1 and 2 Scott Street, December 1924. The posters on the building in the centre provide us with a record of a number of the places to which people could go to enjoy a few hours of leisure – a dance at the Public Hall, a programme of films including Tom Mix at the Apollo Cinema and the turkey drive at Fairbairn Hall.

Freemasons Road in 1953. Badly bombed during the Blitz, the street has yet to be redeveloped. The Kelly's London Directory for 1953 lists the buildings shown here on the west side; 19 - Post Office; 25 - J. Lambert, butcher, 27 - William Ladlow, greengrocer; 29 - Harry Larkin, confectioner. The Larkin family owned a number of shops in East Ham and West Ham. The firm, which still trades, sold peanuts and manufactured a large range of sweets. These buildings were demolished and replaced by a block of shops and flats, namely Normandy Terrace.

Opposite above: Ford's Park Road, from the corner of St. Thomas' Road, 1952.

Opposite below: Plymouth Road, looking north from Fords Park Road in 1952.

A view of Mortlake Road in 1954, includes a row of prefabricated houses.

Children playing in Mortlake Road in the 1950s were usually untroubled by cars.

A few of the houses in Garvary Road, off Prince Regent Lane, in 1970, which had survived the Second World War.

Hartington Road, looking east from Freemasons Road, towards Devonshire Road, c. 1953.

Looking north along Prince Regent Lane in 1902 while the ditch between Saxleby and Garvary Roads was being filled in. Originally Trinity Marsh Lane, it was extended to the Thames around 1811 and served the Charlton ferry which ran until 1844. Canning Town Recreation Ground, commonly known as Beckton Road Park, is on the far left and the Nottingham Arms is on the right.

Three

Schooldays

The Hallsville National School in an engraving from the *Illustrated London News*, 1857. It was originated in 1848, when the vicar of Plaistow opened a class in a shed in Hallsville Road. It met the needs of a population attracted by the new industries and the docks.

This building in Barking Road opened in 1861 as the new Hallsville National School. It later became the Holy Trinity School and was closed in 1940. By 1972 it was a tobacco warehouse and now provides the site for a McDonalds fast-food restaurant.

South Hallsville Senior Boys' School handicraft room, 1936.

Physical training in the hall of the South Hallsville Senior Girls' School, 1936.

The first class, teachers and student teachers at Russell Road Higher Elementary School c. 1906. When the West Ham Secondary School (later Stratford Grammar) opened in Tennyson Road, the pupil teacher centre at Russell Road became a higher elementary school with entry solely by scholarship from elementary schools.

The school shop at the Rosetta Road Infants School in 1936.

The Rosetta County Primary School football team proudly display trophies won in the West Ham Schools Junior Championship and the Junior Football Cup. Football was particularly encouraged in West Ham's schools and some of the boys went on to play for Clapton Football Club and West Ham United.

Beckton Road Infants School, 1922.

The Keir Hardie County Primary School, soon after it had replaced the Beckton Road school in 1952.

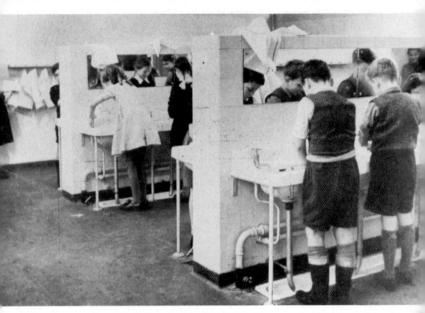

The washroom of the Hallsville Primary School in Radland Road on the Keir Hardie Estate soon after it was rebuilt in 1948.

An open-air lesson at Pretoria Road Senior Boys School in 1936. Built as a modern senior school in 1932, it now forms part of the Eastlea Community School.

The Mayor and Mayoress of West Ham (Alderman and Mrs G.J. Stokes) at a Pretoria Road School party in February 1945. The room is now the community hall of Eastlea School.

Above: Star Lane School, 1927. Amongst its most famous pupils were the actor, Reg Varney, who is best known for his role as Stan Butler in the television series, 'On the Buses', and the singer and actor, David Essex.

Left: Mr Percy Dunlop, a teacher at Star Lane school who, at 83, was the oldest teacher in the country in 1972.

Four

At Work

Above: A barbers, grocers and public house in Bidder Street in 1891. Old Canning Town had a distinct village atmosphere at this time.

Left: A chemists and dispensary at Aberdeen House, Freemasons Road, 1891. As with some other dispensaries, vaccinations and dentistry were also practised at the site, but unusually it was open for two hours every Sunday.

Right: A pawnbrokers in Freemasons Road in 1891. Pawnbrokers were a major source of credit in the area especially when times were hard, as they often were.

Below: E.J. Stone's shop at 231 Barking Road, at its the corner with Star Lane c. 1895. The flour prices displayed in the window are per quartern, a now redundant measure of three-and-a-half pounds, a quarter of a stone.

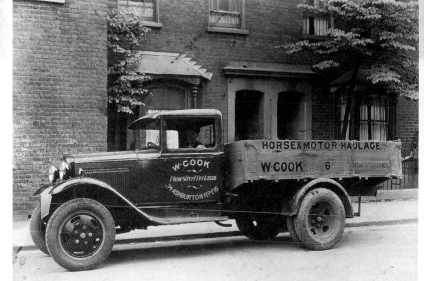

Sankey & Son in the 1930s. Established by 1878, it was a large builders' merchant at Essex Wharf by Canning Town Bridge.

Opposite above: Numbers 1 and 1a Beckton Road, *c.* 1930. Parietti and Bianchi's cafe and dining rooms, one of several Italian-run catering businesses in the area, which included Caldori's.

Opposite below: Mr W. Cook's delivery van in the 1930s.

An automatic self-clamping guillotine at Lamson Paragon, office stationery manufacturers, 1927. Opened in 1893, it was one of the largest employers in Canning Town.

Right: The St. John's Road entrance to the City Glass Bottle Co. which made bottles and jars from 1890 to 1953.

Below: The re-planning of West Ham after the Second World War sought to remove factories from residential areas and the Glass factory was demolished in 1955. Houses on the Keir Hardie Estate can be seen in the background.

A funeral in Canning Town draws the crowds at the turn of the century. Residents made weekly insurance payments to prevent the indignity of a pauper's funeral. Horse-drawn funerals are still sometimes seen in the area.

Opposite above: The entrance to Canning Town Station in Stephenson Street.

Opposite below: Canning Town Fire Station at the corner of Barking and Liverpool Roads, March 1926. It was replaced by a new station in Prince Regent Lane in 1931.

The Railway Station

West Ham 'A' Power Station under construction in January 1903. Built on the site of the Council's sewage works, it replaced the Abbey Mills station and came into operation in 1904. The first electricity generator was housed in the Public Hall, serving the Hall, Canning Town Library, the first Mansfield House residence and a shop in 1895.

Opposite above: West Ham 'A' Power Station. Staff transmitting an order from the Control Room to the Engine Room. One of a series of photographs taken by West Ham Electricity Department in 1937.

Opposite below: West Ham 'B' Power Station. Opened in 1951, on the site of the earlier building, to meet the increased demand for electricity for both domestic and industrial purposes. It had two 280-feet high chimneys and was equipped with the latest coal-handling plant which could receive deliveries either by barges or by rail.

The old market was swept away in the 1960s and replaced by a new market in the Barking Road in 1963. Despite the apparent crowds at the market in 1977, supermarket competition had taken its toll and the market had lost much of its atmosphere.

Opposite above: Rathbone Street Market, 1925. A typical East End market, Rathbone Street bustled until after ten o'clock on a Saturday night. All manner of goods were plied, including medicines such as Rowlands herbal tablets, which are advertised in this picture.

Opposite below: Little remained of Rathbone Street and the surrounding area as a result of the Second World War but the market still thrived in the 1950s.

Preliminary construction work on Canning Town Bridge in 1932. The Bridge House public house can be seen in the middle of the picture and Canning Town Fire Station to its right.

Opposite above: W.W. Howard Bros. Timber Yard, on the corner of Stephenson Street, opposite Canning Town Station, *c.* 1902. Notice the circular iron urinal, less famous than its cousin outside the Connaught Tavern, in Connaught Road.

Opposite below: West Ham Outfall Works at Bow Creek *c.* 1900. West Ham Local Board of Health was installing a sewerage system after the damning Board of Health report, drawn up by Alfred Dickens (Charles' brother) in 1855 and were promised access to the projected North Outfall Sewer. This was later refused, precipitating the use of this works and the River Lea from 1861 until 1901. In 1893 Parliament had granted the new county borough powers to use the Northern Outfall but the necessary work was not completed until 1901.

This northward view shows the Royal Mail Parcelforce international sorting office in Stephenson Street.

Five

The Thames Ironworks

Above: An engraving from the Illustrated London News of Mare & Co.'s Shipbuilding Works, 1854. From 1846 it occupied both the Essex and Middlesex banks of the River Lea. Following Charles Mare's bankruptcy, his father-in-law, Peter Rolt, took over and formed the Thames Ironworks, Shipbuilding and Engineering Company.

Left: Arnold Hills, who joined the board of directors of the Works in 1880 at the age of twenty-three. He later became its Chairman and Managing Director until the firm's closure in 1912.

The visit of the King of Sweden to the Works on 17 May 1900. By this time the company was building for many nations.

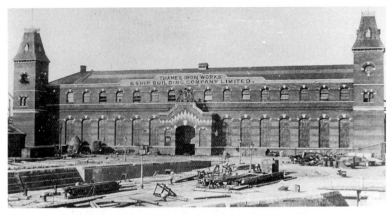

The facade of the general office in 1903, showing the main slipway.

An illustration from the *Thames Ironworks Gazette* of six of the 206 lifeboats built for the Royal National Lifeboat Institution between 1896 and 1911.

The HMS *Albion* in the Victoria Dock in 1900.

A memorial in East London Cemetery to the thirty-eight people who drowned at the launch of the HMS *Albion* on 21 June 1898. They were standing on unsuitable staging and were swept into the water by the wash of the boat.

The HMS *Duncan*, ready for launching into Bow Creek, March 1901.

Opposite above: Romanian torpedo vedette boats, 1906. The Works supplied vessels for a number of navies which were sometimes pitted against each other.

Opposite below: The company also diversified into motor road vehicles as shown by this exhibition stand at Olympia in 1906.

General office staff, 1906. Discipline was tight at the Works, as the faces of the seated management testify. The commissioner, at the back on the right, proudly bears medals probably won in the Boer War.

Drafting the plans for the *Thunderer*. From labourers to civil engineers, the company was one of the area's major employers.

The Ironworks' last ship, the *Thunderer*, was launched on 1 February 1911. Competition from northern yards and rising costs forced the firm's closure in 1912, which caused widespread distress in Canning Town.

The Thames Ironworks Rowing Club, 1898. In addition to promoting shorter working hours and profit sharing, Arnold Hills encouraged his employees to become involved in the company's many social and sporting activities.

The West Ham Memorial Ground was laid out by Hills for the recreation of his staff and to commemorate Queen Victoria's Diamond Jubilee in 1897. The circular track was a major attraction for cyclists and motor-cyclists.

The officials and prizes at the August Bank Holiday sports at the Memorial Grounds in 1898.

The cast of the operatic society's performance of 'The Pirates of Penzance' in 1896.

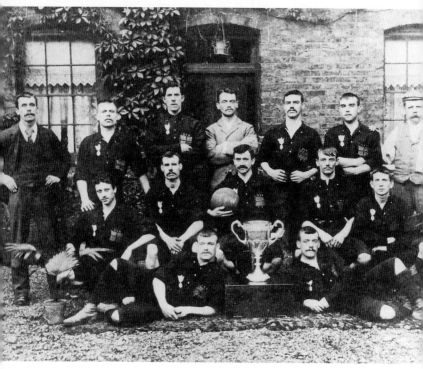

The Thames Ironworks Football Club, 1896. The team had been formed in the previous year with Hills' backing. Originally based at Hermit Road, they played at the Memorial Ground from 1897 until 1904 when they moved to the Boleyn Ground in Green Street. By this time the side had become professional and had been called West Ham United since 1900.

Six

Leisure

Celebrations for King George V's Silver Jubilee in Hoy Street, 6 May 1935. The former Red Lion public house can be seen on the left while St. Luke's Church is in the background.

A group of local residents gathered outside the former Red Lion public house on the corner of Hoy Street and Emily Street.

The celebrations in Nelson Street.

Another picture in Nelson Street. Local photographer, George Taylor, who lived in New Barn Street, Plaistow, took nearly a hundred photographs of the Silver Jubilee celebrations. They are a unique record of the event and a way of life that was to disappear as a result of the Second World War.

Laying the foundation stone of the Public Hall and Canning Town Library in the Barking Road, 1892. The Library opened in 1893 and was the first permanent public library in West Ham. The Public Hall, which opened in the following year, was built as the Town Hall for the southern part of West Ham. Will Thorne, a worker at Beckton Gasworks organised and spoke at the inaugural meeting of the National Union of Gasworkers and General Labourers which was held on the site of these buildings on 31 March 1889.

Right: The Public Hall in the Barking Road, decorated for the West Ham Borough Jubilee in 1936. At this time the Hall was still a centre of social and political activity with boxing, plays, organ recitals and meetings held there regularly. It later became an adult education centre. After a period of closure it was opened by Community Links in 1993 as a community centre.

Below: Canning Town Library, 1955. Hit by a bomb in the Second World War, forty years' issues of *The Times* newspaper, stored in an attic, fanned a blaze which destroyed the Library's roof. The Library was repaired and re-opened in 1954.

Above: A school party using the gramophone record library, 1946. Canning Town Library was also the music library for West Ham, developed after the war by Charles Keyte, the librarian, who was a keen musician. The picture shows C.A.J. Smith, the sub-librarian.

Left: The music section gave Canning Town Library a unique atmosphere and it was a popular place for young people.

Custom House Library in Prince Regent Lane, 1972. Opened in 1905, it was given by Andrew Carnegie, who had opened the Passmore Edwards Library in Plaistow two years before.

An outing from the Sidney Arms in Alice Street, 1930. Public houses were the centre of social activity in the area which had little other recreational facilities – clubs and societies often met in them.

Right: The New Imperial on the Barking Road prepares for its grand re-opening on 15 May 1939. It was renamed the Essoldo in 1958, became a bingo hall in 1963 and was demolished in 1967.

Below: The interior of the Imperial.

BEFORE ALTERATION

Above: St Luke's Church in 1971. Opened in 1875 and known as the 'Cathedral of the East End', the church and its clergy, especially Father Goose, has a special place in the hearts of local people. The building was damaged during the Second World War and subsequently repaired. It was closed in 1985 due to a decline in attendance. Saved from demolition in 1993 as a result of local pressure, there are plans to convert it into a training and community centre.

Left: St. Luke's Church was surrounded by water when the Thames flooded in 1953.

The Boyd Institute, which stood opposite the Church in Tarling (formerly Boyd) Road until its demolition in 1984. It was named after Henry Boyd, Vicar of St. Mark's, Silvertown, who planned St. Luke's Church.

Left: Holy Trinity Church on the corner of the Barking Road and Hermit Road. Opened in 1867, opposite Holy Trinity School (see page 40), it is remembered for the unusually high number of marriages which took place there. Bus conductors, stopping outside, often sang the first line of the music hall song, 'At Trinity Church I met my doom', instead of calling the stop. Damaged during the blitz it re-opened in 1942 and services were held until 1948. It was demolished in 1957 the flats of Trinity Gardens now stand on part of the site.

Below: St. Matthias Church, Hermit Road, *c.* 1910. Opened in 1907, the church was demolished around 1984 and a new church and housing now stand on the site.

The first St. Cedd's church in Beckton Road, originally a mission of St. Andrew's Church Plaistow. It was replaced by a new red-brick church, in 'Romanesque'style, in 1939 as a memorial to 'Tom' Varney, the first Curate. Varney's nephew, John, became the first vicar.

The interior of St. Cedd's from the same date. Like several other churches in south West Ham, St. Cedd's tended to be 'high' church while those in the north-west of the borough tended to be 'low'.

St. Margaret's Roman Catholic Church, Barking Road, 1969. An iron chapel was opened in 1859 and this building was consecrated in 1919.

The Corpus Christi ceremony in the grounds of St. Margaret's convent on Bethell Avenue, 20 June 1954.

The original buildings of St. Margaret's Convent, Bethell Avenue which were built in 1902. The building shown has been converted into an old people's home and is now called St. Margaret's Home.

The interior of St. Margaret's Convent Chapel during the Benediction service, following the Induction of Father K. Heenan as parish priest.

The Peculiar People's Church, Cliff Street. The term 'peculiar people' is derived from the *Book of Deuteronomy* and refers to their practice of isolation from the rest of society. Many members of the sect lived in Edward and Fisher Streets and worked in exclusive gangs at Beckton Gasworks.

On the right of this 1973 view of Star Lane is Tyrell Hall. It was a German Methodist Church serving the local German population who had moved from Whitechapel in the 1870s and worked in the sugar refineries or traded, primarily as butchers and bakers. It closed during the First World War and then became a Methodist-type chapel before being purchased by the Peculiar People in the 1920s.

The Wesleyan Methodist Church on the corner of the Barking Road and Ordnance Road before the First World War. The Poplar-based seamen's mission, the Queen Victoria Seamen's Rest organised a number of activities here, including the Coloured People's Institute which was opened in the 1930s to serve black seamen, many of whom lived with their families in Canning Town and Custom House. Badly damaged on the first day of the Blitz, 7 September 1940, it was subsequently demolished.

Left: St. Anne's Roman Catholic Church, Berwick Road which opened in 1899. The building has been demolished and a new church stands on the site.

Below: Canning Town Synagogue, the Barking Road. It was built in 1923 to serve the large Jewish population, many of whom traded in Rathbone Street market or ran shops in the Barking and Victoria Dock Roads. Congregation numbers fell after the Second World War as many Jews moved away to live in Essex. Although derelict in this photograph from 1984, it was renovated and is now a Muslim Community Centre.

Seven

Social Action

Left: Canning Town became the focus of trade union and political activity as people fought for improvements in their working conditions and sought to hold office on the local council and in Parliament. Elected in 1892 as the first truly independent Labour MP James Keir Hardie soon became known as the 'Member for the Unemployed'. He was the first chairman of the Parliamentary Labour Party, founded in 1906, and spoke at a number of meetings at the Public Hall in Canning Town.

Below: Local MP Elwyn Jones and Councillor A. Wolffe, Chairman of the Public Libraries Committee, with a representative of the Independent Labour Party, admire the bust of Keir Hardie at an exhibition at the Public Hall in 1956 to mark the centenary of his birth. The bust had been presented to West Ham in 1948 and was put on display at Canning Town Library.

Looking north from the site of the Keir Hardie Estate towards the City Glass Bottle Works and the Paragon Works.

Looking west from the Lamson Paragon Works along Elphick Street, 28 September 1945.

Some of the first houses to be opened on the Keir Hardie Estate on Appleby Road in April 1947. One of the largest areas of re-development in the country, the Keir Hardie Estate was built on a site which had been heavily bombed during the Second World War. The Estate was planned as a neighbourhood unit which included traditional 'garden city' accommodation, schools, shops and community and health services.

A children's playground near Victoria Dock Road, seen in September 1951, was one of the many new facilities on the Keir Hardie Estate.

Inhabitants of the Keir Hardie estate wade knee-deep through the floods which resulted from the collapse of the river wall by the site of the Thames Ironworks in January 1953.

Mothers and babies made homeless by the 1953 floods were supplied with food and soup at the rest centre in the Public Hall.

Devonshire Road, February 1936. New housing was built during the 1930s in the Prince Regent Lane area, on one of the last undeveloped sites in West Ham.

Opposite above: Some of the sixty-two new houses completed in Murray Square, off Coolfin Road, Custom House, in March 1951.

Opposite below: Examples of the post-war flats built around Liverpool and Dale Roads, north of the Barking Road in September 1951.

Right: Less expensive to build than traditional houses and accommodating large numbers of people, tower blocks were seen to be the ideal solution to the housing shortage. A number of them were built in Canning Town and Custom House in the 1960s, including Ronan Point in Butchers Road. A gas cooker lit on the eighteenth floor of that block, early on the morning of 16 May 1968, resulted in an explosion which caused the collapse of part of the corner of the building.

Below: The emergency and rescue services with the assistance of workers from the docks, used bulldozers and cranes to clear the rubble and search for anyone trapped. Four of the 260 people living in Ronan Point were killed (a fifth victim died several days later) and the injured were taken to hospital. The disaster was headline news and photographs of the collapsed block dominated the front pages of newspapers around the world. Ronan Point became a by-word for the failure of the post-war dream of high-rise living.

Above: Empty and decaying, the tower blocks in the Freemasons Road area stand starkly against the skyline in November 1987. They soon met the fate of Ronan Point which was demolished in 1986, to be replaced by houses.

Right: Children play in the shadow of the tower blocks.

Left: Will Thorne. A lifelong member of the Social Democratic Federation, he founded the Gas and General Labourers Union in 1889 which developed into the present General Municipal and Boilermakers Union. He was a member of West Ham Council from 1891 to 1946 and its Mayor from 1917–1918. He was Labour MP for South West Ham from 1906–1918 and the new constituency of Plaistow 1918–1945. He was a familiar figure at the local speaker's corner at the junction of the Barking Road and Beckton Road.

Below: A convoy with police escort during the General Strike in May 1926 passes along Prince Regent Lane in front of Shipman Road School.

Above: A policeman sits besides the driver in a steam-powered lorry in the convoy.

Right: A cartoon of Jack Jones, MP for Silvertown from 1918 to 1940. Lloyd George thought Jones to be one of the wittiest men in the House, a contrast to Will Thorne, who was a more pedestrian speaker.

Daisy Parsons giving milk to needy babies in Fife Road in 1914. Although damaged, this rare photograph gives a valuable insight into the important early work of the suffragette movement. Parsons was an active member of the local branch of the East London Federation of Suffragettes and worked alongside its leader, Sylvia Pankhurst, on a number of campaigns.

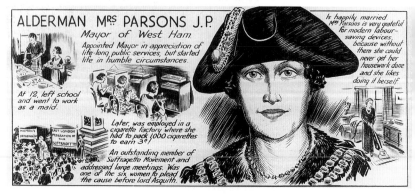

A pictorial record of Daisy Parsons' life from the age of twelve to her election as the first woman Mayor of West Ham in 1936. Mrs. Parsons was awarded an M.B.E. for her public service in 1951 and died in 1957.

By now the Mayor of West Ham, Daisy Parsons is seen with Pat Dennahy at the opening of Beckton Lido, 30 August 1937.

Councillors Bill Gillman, left and David Thorogood accompany Mrs Parsons for this less formal photograph.

Daisy Parsons and her daughter bump a councillor on a boundary stone during the perambulation of the West Ham Borough boundaries in May 1937. West Ham 'A' power station can be seen in the background.

Opposite above: HRH Princess Mary (the Princess Royal) lays the foundation stone of the Chapel of Saint Helena at the Dockland Settlement, 1929. Members of Malvern College, at that time a public school, set up the settlement in 1894. They aimed to provide social improvement through the encouragement of sport, culture and Christian values.

Opposite below: The swimming baths at the Dockland Settlement in 1930.

DOCKLAND SETTLEMENT SWIMMING BATH.

Prince Philip, the Duke of Edinburgh and Mayor Hearn meet young boxers at the Dockland Settlement in 1947. Boxing was encouraged at many of the settlements.

Opposite above: Princess Margaret, one of several members of the Royal Family to take an interest in the work of the settlement, visits in June 1952.

Opposite below: Celebrities were also regular visitors. Wilfred Pickles, the broadcaster, is shown here introducing Esta Bailey and John Sadler, two young singers.

This is a vivid picture of 1950s, with some slogans that would not seem out of place on contemporary marches.

Opposite above: A Communist Party meeting near the junction of Beckton Road and the Barking Road in July 1952. Holy Trinity Church can be seen in the background.

Opposite below: The speaker is Harry Pollitt, the well-known Communist leader.

The opening of the Beckton Road Children's Home in 1954. Alderman Sullivan is holding the train while the Mayor, Mrs Harris, is on the left and Mr Baker the Children's officer is on the far right.

Children play outside the Beckton Road Children's Home.

Eight

The War Years

Peace celebrations in Kerry Street, a poor street off Victoria Dock Road, probably in July 1919. The Mansfield House Magazine drew attention to what they saw as an 'unpleasant' feature of the celebrations – 'the number of girls and young women masquerading in male apparel, civil as well as naval and military'.

Opposite above: During the First World War German Zeppelins and aircraft brought war to the Home Front. Leo Grogan, aged seven, was killed as a result of the injuries he received when a bomb dropped by a German aircraft in one of the last air raids of the War hit his house at 12 Ladysmith Road on 18 May 1918.

Opposite below: Crowds gather around the funeral carriage in Ladysmith Road.

"PEACE CELEBRATIONS" GAMBUS RD 19.7.1919   Nº6

"PEACE CELEBRATIONS" GAMBUS RD 19.7.1919   Nº5

PEACE CELEBRATIONS CAMBUS RD 19·7·1919

In contrast to Kerry Street, Cambus Road was a better-off working class area. It was a private landlord development of upstairs and downstairs flats, each with its own front door.

Opposite above: Peace celebrations on the Cambus Road, 19 July 1919. Two members of the Allen family from 35 Cambus Road can be seen on the second row, Edward James is fifth from the left while Barbara is third from the right.

Opposite below: This photograph from the same series includes a black woman in the second row. The majority of black people in Canning Town at this time lived in the streets off Victoria Dock Road.

ARP (Air Raid Precautions) members assess the night's damage in Beckton Road and how best to deal with it.

Opposite above: Children come out to see the houses in Mortlake Road which had been damaged by bombs on 6 September 1940, the day before the Blitz on London began. South Molton and Beckton Road were also damaged (see below).

Opposite below: Air-raid wardens, rescue parties and the emergency services were sent out from the Control Centre to deal with this bomb incident in South Molton Road. A member of the Home Guard with his rifle is on duty.

Seven firemen were killed when their sub-station at Gainsborough Road received a direct hit on 8 December 1940. Fire-fighting appliances conveyed their coffins in the funeral procession along Hermit Road to East London Cemetery where they were buried on 17 December 1940. Two of the firemen – Gage and Hammersley – are remembered in the street names in Canning Town.

Opposite above: South Hallsville School was being used as a rest centre by hundreds of people who had been bombed out their houses in Canning Town. It was devastated during the air raid on 10 September 1940. Debate continues on the number of people killed, the official estimate was seventy-three. The Lamson Paragon Works can be seen behind the school on the right.

Opposite below: Beckton Road school was damaged and the windows blown out when a bomb struck on 18 April 1941.

Timber salvaged from the bomb-damaged houses was stored at this depot in Nelson Street in 1942 and used for repairing and re-building others. The spire of St. Luke's can be seen in the background.

A stock-pile of doors at the Prince Regent Lane depot in 1942.